SONORAN DESERT

For Aubrey, as always,
and to editor Kristen McCurry and designer
Lois Rainwater, who have made
the series stronger.

—W. L.

Copyright © 2009 by Rowman & Littlefield Publishing Group, Inc.
Photography © 2009 by Wayne Lynch
p. 10: Chihuahuan desert photo, Hobbs Photo Images © Jared Hobbs;
p. 56: ringtail photo © Joe Van Os
Map illustration by Mary Jo Scibetta
Design by Lois A. Rainwater

NORTHWORD
Books for Young Readers

Published by Taylor Trade Publishing
An imprint of The Rowman & Littlefield Publishing Group, Inc.
4501 Forbes Boulevard, Suite 200, Lanham, Maryland 20706
www.rlpgtrade.com

Estover Road, Plymouth PL6 7PY, United Kingdom

Distributed by NATIONAL BOOK NETWORK

Library of Congress Cataloging-in-Publication Data

Lynch, Wayne.
Sonoran Desert / text and photographs by Wayne Lynch ; assisted by Aubrey Lang.
p. cm. — (Our wild world ecosystems)
Includes index.
ISBN-13: 978-1-58979-389-7 (cloth : alk. paper)
ISBN-10: 1-58979-389-7 (cloth : alk. paper)
1. Natural history—Sonoran Desert—Juvenile literature. 2. Ecology—Sonoran Desert—Juvenile
literature. 3. Natural history—Sonoran Desert—Pictorial works—Juvenile literature.
4. Ecology—Sonoran Desert—Pictorial works—Juvenile literature.
5. Sonoran Desert—Environmental conditions—Juvenile literature.
6. Sonoran Desert—Pictorial works—Juvenile literature. I. Lang, Aubrey. II. Title.

QH104.5.S58L96 2009

577.5409791'7—dc22   2008036635

The paper used in this publication meets the minimum requirements of
American National Standard for Information Sciences—
Permanence of Paper for Printed Library Materials, ANSI/NISO Z39.48-1992.

Printed in China

SONORAN DESERT

Text and Photographs by Wayne Lynch
Assisted by Aubrey Lang

NORTHWORD
Taylor Trade Publishing
Lanham • New York • Boulder • Toronto • Plymouth, UK

CONTENTS

One spring, 25 years ago, I was part of a three-person team collecting rattlesnakes in the deserts of northern Mexico for the University of Arizona. As we were driving back to the United States border we were stopped by police with machine guns at a roadblock. My two friends and I had just spent a week camping and crawling around the hot desert. I wasn't surprised when the police pulled us over because none of us had washed or shaved during that time and we looked like real troublemakers. We had caught a number of rattlesnakes for the university and we had the live snakes in cloth bags inside a Styrofoam cooler on the back seat. The snakes shared the cooler with a block of stale cheese, some moldy bread, and a few wrinkled sticks of salami. The police were probably looking for drug smugglers and, unfortunately, as filthy as we were, we looked the type. Normally, stories involving machine guns, smelly biologists, and dangerous rattlesnakes do not end well. As it turned out, the police checked every inch of our car, but to our amazement they never checked the cooler on the back seat. As we drove away we joked that the police probably thought the food in our cooler would smell worse than we did.

THE DESERT WORLD

THE DESERTS OF THE WORLD cover over a quarter of the land on Earth. If you search for the word desert in different dictionaries you will see that it is used to describe a barren, uninteresting, worthless place. How wrong that is! Deserts are not empty, boring wastelands, but exciting wild areas filled with fascinating animals and plants, often found nowhere else.

AUSTRALIAN DESERT

NAMIB DESERT

SAHARA DESERT

All deserts have two things in common: hot temperatures and low rainfall. If you look at a map of the world you will notice that most of the deserts occur in two bands, north and south of the Equator. South of the Equator, there is the great Australian Desert, which covers half of Australia. Here, there is a greater variety of lizards and venomous snakes than anywhere else in the world.

EQUATOR: an imaginary line that circles the earth like a belt, halfway between the North and South poles

Also south of the Equator you will find the Namib Desert of Africa with its monster-size sand dunes that reach over 900 feet (274 m) high, and the Atacama Desert of South America, which is the driest desert in the world. In some areas of the Atacama it may rain only once in ten years.

VENOMOUS: an animal that injects a toxin through fangs, barbs, or a stinger

North of the Equator there are the great deserts of Central Asia as well as the magnificent Sahara Desert of Africa where violent blowing sandstorms can sometimes make the days as dark as night. The Sahara, which is as big as the United States, is the largest desert in the world. Also north of the Equator are the beautiful deserts of North America.

The large red rocks, called the Olgas, are in the center of the Australian Desert. The area is sacred to the native Aboriginal people. In the past, in the Namib Desert, native peoples such as the Bushman would sometimes hunt for antelopes in the dunes. And in the Sahara Desert, the Tuareg people would travel great distances over dunes by riding on camels.

Four different deserts occur in the United States and northern Mexico. The most northern of these is the Great Basin Desert, which is bounded by the Rocky Mountains in the east and by the Cascade and Sierra Nevada Mountains in the west. The Great Basin Desert gets most of its moisture in winter when it snows. Very few cactuses grow here, and the most common plant is a strong-smelling bush called sagebrush.

The Mojave (mo-HAHV-ee) Desert in California and southern Nevada is the smallest of the four deserts. The typical plant of the Mojave is the Joshua tree. This tree, which can grow up to 40 feet (12 m) tall, has shaggy bark and long, stiff, pointed leaves. Most of this desert receives less than 5 inches (13 cm) of rain a year. The most famous place in the Mojave Desert is Death Valley, which holds the record for the hottest temperature ever reported in the United States, a sizzling 134°F (57°C). At this temperature, an adult man resting in the shade would sweat so much that he would need to drink more than 9 quarts (8.5 l) of water a day just to survive.

The sagebrush bushes of the Great Basin Desert usually grow just 2 to 4 feet (0.6–1.2 m) high, but in some places they can be up to 7 feet (2.1 m) in height.

The Joshua trees of the Mojave Desert are home to many desert creatures. Hawks, owls, doves, and other birds nest in their branches, while lizards, scorpions, and mice often live under their shaggy bark.

The Chihuahuan (CHEE-wah-wahn) Desert is found mostly in northern Mexico, but a small portion of it is located in the southern parts of Texas and New Mexico. The Chihuahuan Desert occurs farther south than the other North American deserts and it gets most of its rainfall in summer. One group of plants that is typical of this desert is the agaves (ah-GAHV-ays). The thick fleshy leaves of agave plants were very important to the early Indians. They roasted the leaves for food, dried them to make ropes, rugs, and baskets, and soaked them to make the famous alcoholic drink called tequila (teh-KEE-la).

You will have noticed already that many words used in describing the desert are pronounced in an unusual way. That's because the words are Spanish and have a Spanish pronunciation.

GREAT BASIN

MOJAVE

SONORAN

CHIHUAHUAN

The Chihuahuan Desert is protected in Big Bend National Park in southern Texas. The low green plants at the bottom of the photograph are a type of agave that is sometimes called shin dagger. The thick leaves have a very sharp point that can stab you in the ankles and legs if you are not careful.

Left: The four deserts of North America.

Once a saguaro cactus reaches a height of 15 to 20 feet (4.5–6 m) it starts to grow branches, called arms. A large saguaro may have five or more arms.

The Sonoran Desert, the last of the sun-baked four, forms a horseshoe around the upper end of the Gulf of California. A large part of this desert is in northwestern Mexico, but it also crosses the border into Arizona and southern California. The Sonoran Desert has more wildflowers, more kinds of spiny cactuses, more lizards and snakes, and more spiders, scorpions, and other creepy crawlies than any of the other deserts in North America. The symbol of the Sonoran Desert is the gigantic saguaro (sah-WAH-row) cactus that can grow more than 50 feet (15 m) tall. I have been lucky enough to travel to every desert in the world, but for all of these reasons, the Sonoran is my favorite.

SUNBATHERS:
DESERT WILDLIFE

The mixture of animals and birds that live in the desert are quite different from those that live in the prairie grasslands, in the wetlands of the Florida Everglades, or on the treeless tundra of the Arctic. The heat and dryness of the desert is a challenge for many animals, yet some do well and are plentiful. Others have a difficult time and are scarce. For example, because there is so little water in the desert, amphibians, such as frogs, toads, and salamanders, which rely on water, are uncommon. On the other hand, scaly-skinned reptiles such as snakes and lizards, which like the heat and need much less water than amphibians, are among the most common residents of the desert. Insects, spiders, scorpions, centipedes, and other small animals are also especially common in the desert.

The mammals of the desert are mostly small ones such as mice, kangaroo rats, wood rats, and pocket gophers. These small mammals can escape the heat by digging tunnels underground. There are no large herds of mammals such as buffalo or elk grazing in the desert as there are in the prairie grasslands because there is not enough grass for them to eat. There are more small mammals because small mammals require less food to sustain themselves than large ones, and generally, food is seasonal in deserts and of limited supply.

Top: The harmless gopher snake is one of the largest snakes in the Sonoran Desert, growing to lengths of 9 feet (2.7 m). It hunts mainly small mammals and birds.

Middle: These ants were working together to move a fallen ocotillo flower that was blocking the entrance to the colony's underground nest.

Bottom: The pocket gopher gets its name from the fur-lined pockets it has on either side of its mouth. It uses these pockets to carry extra food.

MIGRATION: when a bird or animal moves to a new area with the change of seasons

When it comes to birds, the desert has some species (SPEE-cies), or kinds, that live there only during the winter months when it is cooler while others can nest even during the hottest summer months. However, more than half of the birds that are found in the desert are only temporary visitors. They pass through the desert in the spring and autumn during migration, when they travel between their summer breeding areas in the north and their winter homes farther south.

This gila woodpecker was feeding on the insects in the center of a prickly pear cactus flower.

This book is a different kind of nature book than you may have read before. It's a book about an ecosystem, the Sonoran Desert ecosystem. Ecosystem is the word scientists use to describe all of the plants and animals that live together in a community. It is also about how the soil, the warmth of the days, and the amount of rain affects these animals and plants. In an ecosystem, all these things are connected and work together. The Sonoran Desert ecosystem is a story about toads that listen for thunder and coyotes that howl at the stars. It is a story about tortoises that eat cactuses, bighorn sheep that rarely drink, and owls that burrow underground. It is also a tale about sand dunes and desert floods, lizards that swim through sand, and spiders as big as saucers.

Some people might call me a "cactus hugger" because I love the desert so much. My first experience with the Sonoran Desert was in Baja, Mexico, more than 25 years ago. Since then I have returned many times to different areas in the Sonoran, and each time I see something new and exciting. On my last visit, for example, I found four different kinds of owls, a black and yellow snake that burrows in the sand, and a beautiful black and pink gila (HEE-lah) monster—a venomous lizard—all in the same day. With this book I hope to share with you some of the beauty of the Sonoran Desert and the many clever ways that the plants and animals make their living.

The night sky never looks more beautiful than in the desert. Because the air in the desert is so dry and clear and there are usually no clouds, the stars look like bright glittering diamonds in the velvet blackness of the sky. I remember many winter nights when I slept on the ground to watch the sky and listen to the desert. Years later, I still remember how happy I felt when I heard the familiar hooting of a great horned owl, the soft thud of a kangaroo rat hopping across the ground nearby, and the distant howl of a coyote. Even the gentle whisper of the wind through the bushes always makes me smile. How often do we really listen to the world around us? In the desert at night, sounds travel far and they can tell you many interesting stories if you are willing to listen.

HOT AND THIRSTY

WATER IS THE MOST IMPORTANT liquid in life. Plants are mostly made of water, and without a steady supply of water, all of them eventually wilt and die. A thirsty saguaro cactus, for example, may hold 80 pounds (36 kg) of water in every foot (0.3 m) of its stem. So, a 40-foot (12.2 m) tall saguaro with three or four long arms might hold more than 2 tons (1,814 kg) of water.

How much water do you think is inside your body? Actually, the bodies of all animals, including humans, are mostly made of water. For example, a 10-year-old boy who weighs 80 pounds (36 kg), has at least 50 pounds (23 kg) of water inside his body. If that boy got lost in the desert without any water the situation would soon become very dangerous. In just two days he might sweat enough to lose 4 pounds (2 kg) of water, even if he sat in the shade and didn't move. He wouldn't feel like moving anyway, because the loss of water would make him feel very tired, his eyes would be sore and scratchy because he could no longer produce tears, and his mouth would be as dry as paper. On the third day he might lose 2 more pounds (1 kg) of water and feel very sick and not know where he was. Later that day, even before the sun went down, he would probably die of dehydration once he had lost just 6 pounds (3 kg) of water.

DEHYDRATION: a dangerous condition that results when the body has lost too much water to function normally

Because water is so important to plants and animals, deserts present a special challenge to everything that lives there. Why? Because all the deserts in the world are dry and none of them receives more than 10 or 11 inches (25 cm) of rain in a year. Compare that with the 20 inches (51 cm) of rain that falls on the prairie grasslands in eastern Nebraska, or the 60 inches (152 cm) that soaks the Florida Everglades, or the 33 feet (10 m) of rain that floods the slopes of Mount Waialeale in Hawaii.

Not every part of the Sonoran Desert gets the same amount of rain. The desert is much drier in the west than it is in the east. For example, Tucson, Arizona, in the eastern part of the desert gets about 11 inches (28 cm) of rain every year, whereas Yuma, Arizona, farther west may receive only 4 inches (10 cm). The area around Yuma, however, like everywhere in the desert, doesn't always receive the same amount of rain every year. In some years it may get more than 4 inches (10 cm) while in other years it may get much less. Some years in Yuma it rains less than an inch (2.5 cm) in the whole year. For the plants and animals of the desert this can be deadly dry.

The Gulf of California is a warm finger of the Pacific Ocean reaching into the center of the Sonoran Desert. In the rich waters of the gulf there are dozens of desert islands where brown pelicans, blue-footed boobies, gulls, and terns come to nest. It seems odd to see so many water-loving seabirds in the middle of the desert.

Both the blue-footed booby (left) and the brown pelican are diving seabirds. The pelican hunts near the surface of the water and tries to trap fish inside its large mouth. The booby dives much deeper than the pelican and can reach depths of 20 feet (6 m).

PENINSULA: a finger of land surrounded by water on three sides

When scientists measure the rainfall in a desert they simply measure the total inches that hit the ground in a year. However, 2 inches (5 cm) of rain that wets the desert in the winter is different than 2 inches (5 cm) of rain in the summer. Winter storms in the Sonoran Desert, which happen between December and March, often produce gentle steady rains that may last for several days. When this happens, the rain has time to soak into the ground where the roots of desert plants can drink it up.

On the other hand, rainfall in the summer months of July and August often comes in violent thunderstorms that may dump several inches of rain in less than an hour. When so much rain falls so quickly, the rain doesn't have enough time to soak into the ground and it runs away into creeks and rivers and is lost. When this happens, riverbeds that were once bone dry can suddenly flood with several feet of water from thunderstorms that are miles away. It may seem strange that people could drown in the desert, but they sometimes do when they don't heed the warnings and drive across dry desert rivers that are suddenly struck by these flash floods in summer.

ECO-Fact

The Baja Peninsula, which forms the western edge of the Sonoran Desert, was once attached to the mainland coast of Mexico. Millions of year ago, the crust of the Earth cracked and the peninsula broke away allowing the ocean to flood the land in between. The flooded area is now called the Gulf of California. The crack in the earth, called the San Andreas Fault, is still splitting away today and is the reason there are so many earthquakes in this area.

FLASH FLOOD: a dangerous, sudden surge of water that comes and goes quickly

HOT DAYS
COOL NIGHTS

Dryness is just one of the two important features of a desert. The other important feature is high temperatures. If low rainfall was the only feature of a desert then many areas of the Arctic could also be called deserts because many of them get less than 11 inches (27.9 cm) of rain a year. However, the Arctic is cold and the desert is hot, sometimes very hot. In the Sonoran Desert summer temperatures can reach 120°F (49°C). When the air temperature is that hot the temperature on the surface of the bare ground can be higher than 160°F (71°C), which is hot enough to fry an egg. One day in this kind of heat would be tolerable, but imagine three months where the temperatures are over 100°F (38°C) every day. That's the way it is in the Sonoran Desert every summer.

CLIMATE: the different types of weather that occur in an area

Even though the daytime temperatures in the desert can be baking hot, it's surprising how chilly it can get at night. I can remember many times in the desert when sweat poured off my face in the daytime and at night I needed a sweater and jacket to stay warm. The reason the desert cools off so much at night is because of the dry air. When there is very little moisture in the air, there are no clouds. Without clouds, when the sun goes down at night, the heat of the earth quickly escapes into the dry sky and the temperature falls. In areas where there are clouds, the heat released from the earth bounces off the bottom of the clouds and is reflected back toward the ground. This keeps the nighttime temperature warm so it doesn't cool down as much as it does in the drier climate of the desert.

PLANT TRICKS

Plants are mostly made of water, but they also lose water continuously through tiny holes in their stems and leaves. The plants replace the water they lose by soaking it up with their roots from the soil. However, if the soil is dry, as it often is in the desert, the plants continue to lose water through their leaves and stem every day. If they lose too much water they wilt and die. To keep this from happening, desert plants use special tricks.

One trick that some desert plants use to conserve moisture is to shed their leaves as soon as the soil dries out. Then, if it rains again they grow a new set of leaves in just a few days. This is what the ocotillo (oka-TEE-oh) plant does, and in some years it may grow three or four different crops of leaves.

The sweet sugary water inside the flowers of the ocotillo plant is an important food for hummingbirds.

The leaves of the ocotillo turn red when they dry out and soon afterward fall off.

Another way for desert plants to lose less water through their leaves is to cover them with a waxy coating as the creosote (CREE-oh-sote) plant does. The wax acts like a protective covering to keep the leaf from drying out. The creosote bush is a very tough plant that grows in the driest areas of the desert, each plant growing a good distance from the other so they don't have to compete for water in the soil. The Mexican name for the plant is "little stinker" because the bush gives off a strong smell like medicine, especially after it rains.

Many desert plants are experts at waiting for rain and they do this as seeds. The seeds of some wildflowers may stay buried in the dirt for 25 years until enough rain falls for them to finally grow. How does a desert seed know when there is enough rain for it to start growing? After all, how smart can a seed be anyway? Couldn't a seed get fooled in a year when only a small amount of rain falls on the desert? Then if it tried to grow it would dry up and die before it finished because there wouldn't be enough water for it to produce any flowers and make new seeds. This is where you see how really smart a seed can be.

Creosote is one of the most common bushes in the Sonoran Desert. Some scientists believe that this very successful plant may live longer than any other living thing on earth. One creosote plant near Palm Springs, California, may be more than 11,000 years old, making it thousands of years older than any human civilization.

The Mexican gold poppy blooms in spring after heavy winter rains.

The seeds of many desert wildflowers are covered with a thick coat, like a shell. Inside the shell there is a natural drug that acts like a sleeping pill. The drug keeps the seed waiting and prevents it from growing. Each time it rains, some of the drug gets washed away. Only after it rains a lot and all of the drug gets flushed away will the seed finally wake up and begin to grow. It's as if the seed figured out how wet the ground needs to be for it to have time to grow, sprout flowers, and produce another bunch of seeds.

When the winter rains are earlier and wetter than usual, the seeds of many wildflowers get a chance to grow, and the desert becomes a wonderful carpet of orange poppies, blue lupines,

red spikes of owl clover, and yellow goldfields. This amazing display of color usually happens in March and April every three or four years. The colorful flowers only last for a couple of weeks, but they are so beautiful that people travel to the Sonoran Desert from all over the world to see them. Desert flower-watching in the spring is so popular that many web sites on the internet give regular reports on the flowers and where the best displays can be seen.

Top & Bottom:
The bright yellow flowers of the palo verde (VIR-day) tree can be so numerous they hide the branches. So many bees were feeding on the flowers of this tree you could hear the buzzing sound from 20 feet (6 m) away.

Left: The prickly poppy is a tough plant that doesn't dry out easily. Its seeds are a favorite food of doves. Native peoples of the desert used the plant's bitter sap to treat skin diseases.

THE PORCUPINE PLANTS

When most people think of the desert they think of cactuses. In the Sonoran Desert there are perhaps 300 different kinds of cactuses, which is more than anywhere else in the world. The cactuses have playful names, including beavertail, jumping cholla (CHOY-ah), teddy bear cholla, staghorn cholla, horse crippler, spiny barrel, strawberry hedgehog, pincushion, pancake prickly pear, and fish hook barrel cactus.

Cactuses have a number of ways to survive in the heat and dryness of the desert. First of all, cactus plants have no leaves where water can be lost. As well, the swollen stems and branches of a cactus are covered with a thick wax, which keeps the plant from drying out. The roots of a cactus grow very close to the surface of the ground so that even when it rains just a little the plant can soak up some of the water. If it rains a lot, the cactus can store extra water in the soft spongy inside parts of its branches and stem. But too much water can actually be bad for a cactus. It may store so much water that it swells and splits. If a tall cactus such as a cardón (car-DOHN) or a saguaro stores too much water inside itself it can become top heavy and fall over in a strong wind. The shallow roots of a cactus are little help to keep the waterlogged plant from toppling over.

The flowers of the prickly pear cactus last for just a day or so before they turn a pale orange and fall off.

The flowers of the staghorn cholla cactus can vary in color from red, purple, and orange to pink and yellow. The different colored flowers may grow in the same area of desert.

24

All cactuses have spines. Some spines are long and stiff, others hooked and flat, but all of them are sharp. The spines on the jumping cholla are so sharp that no matter how lightly you touch them they stick into your skin and a piece of the cactus breaks off with them. You are left with a painful pincushion stuck to your hand. I know this, because I have accidentally bumped into the jumping cholla many times. If you try to remove the painful piece of cactus with your other hand it gets stuck, too. The only way to do it is to use a stick and flip the cactus piece loose.

The spines on a cactus not only protect the plant from hungry animals but they also shade the plant from the heat of the sun so that the cactus doesn't get too hot. The teddy bear cholla gets its name because it is covered by so many golden spines that the cactus looks like it is wearing a thick, furry coat. The thick spines are especially good at shading the cholla and keeping it cool.

ECO-Alert

In recent years, so many people have moved to the Sonoran Desert to live and play golf that they have drained much of the underground water. As the water level drops it gets harder and harder for the roots of cottonwood and willow trees to reach the water and the trees eventually die of dehydration. Most of the trees along the Salt, Gila, Santa Cruz, and Rillito Rivers in Arizona have disappeared because their roots can no longer reach the water they need to survive.

ALLUVIAL: an area of fine soil that has been left behind by flowing water

Although the cactuses and wildflowers of the desert are interesting to study, it is wildlife of the Sonoran Desert that I love the best. There are four important wildlife habitats in the Sonoran Desert: the alluvial (aa-LOO-vee-al) plains; sand dunes; rocky slopes called bajadas (bah-HAH-dahs); and desert mountains. In the pages that follow, we'll take a look at the wildlife in each of these four areas. Some desert animals live their entire lives in only one of these habitats. For instance, the fringe-toed lizard lives only in sandy areas. Others, such as the coyote, may wander through all four habitats. So, when I talk about an animal in a certain area, that doesn't mean it can't live anywhere else in the desert.

CHAPTER THREE

"Normally I don't like to interfere with nature but on one trip to the Sonoran Desert, I was glad I did. It was late April, and I had come across a remarkable sight. A large male desert tortoise was courting a female in the sunshine of the morning. The tortoises were so preoccupied with each other that I decided it was a great chance to get some photos without disturbing them. Everything seemed to be going according to plan for the male until it came to the tricky part of balancing on the female's domed shell. The female tortoise continued to walk around, making the male's balancing act even more difficult. Suddenly, the male fell over backwards, landing upside down. He waved his legs violently, but wasn't able to turn himself over. He struggled for about 15 minutes until he was exhausted. The tortoise then seemed to give up and he lay there quietly, helpless. I had a thermometer with me and the ground temperature was 115°F (46°C). As I sat in the shade, I knew the tortoise would soon overheat and die if I didn't come to his rescue and flip him over. I thought about what to do for a few minutes then picked him up and placed him safely, right side up, in the shade of a bush."

DESERT PLAINS AND WASHES

BETWEEN THE DESERT MOUNTAIN chains there are wide, flat valleys called alluvial plains. Creosote bushes grow well in the alluvial soil. These plains cover a greater area of the Sonoran Desert than any other wildlife habitat.

Dry riverbeds, called washes, crisscross the alluvial plains in many areas. During the winter and summer, when it rains, the rivers may flood with water for a short time but most of them eventually dry up again. Many water-loving desert trees grow along the banks of dry washes. The trees wait for the few times each year when there is water in the rivers, and many of the trees have deep roots to reach far underground for water. The dry washes are like winding sandy roads across the desert, and animals often use them to travel from place to place. Because many trees and bushes grow along the edges of a wash and offer shade and hiding places, it is a good spot for lizards, snakes, and birds to live.

DESERT
SLOWPOKE

A tortoise is really just a turtle that lives on dry land away from the water. The desert tortoise lives in some of the driest areas of the Sonoran Desert. The slowpoke tortoise never seems to be in a hurry, which may explain why it lives longer than any other desert creature. Most desert snakes and songbirds live fewer than 10 years. Some bighorn sheep and deer can live to be 15, and the occasional tarantula and large lizard reach 25 years of age. The desert tortoise easily beats them all. Some tortoises live more than 80 years!

A tortoise spends the winter deep inside a burrow, sometimes 30 feet (9 m) long. Other desert animals, including wood rats and rattlesnakes, may share the burrow with it. The desert tortoise comes out of winter hibernation in late March when the spring flowers are blooming and temperatures are starting to warm up. Tortoises, like all reptiles, need the sun to warm their bodies before they have enough energy to move around and eat.

A tortoise's favorite foods are fresh wildflowers and juicy green grasses. The plants allow the tortoise to get fat and store water. In the desert, green plants may dry up quickly so the tortoise must race with time to eat as much food as it can while the plants are still green. In very dry years, a desert tortoise may have only a few weeks when food is plentiful. By October the tortoises are back inside their winter burrows hibernating. This amazing scheme for beating the heat has served the desert tortoise well for millions of years.

HIBERNATION: the deep sleep used by animals to avoid cold weather and to save energy when food is scarce or not available

When a desert tortoise is frightened it pulls its head inside its shell and uses its scaly front legs to shield itself.

ECO-Alert

Some people like to keep desert snakes, lizards, tortoises, and tarantulas as pets. After they are taken from their desert homes, these animals often die because they are not cared for properly. When too many people do this, the animals can disappear completely from the desert.

REPTILE: a scaly, cold-blooded animal

TOADS WITH SHOVELS

Most toads and frogs lay their eggs in water and start life as tadpoles swimming around in puddles and ponds. Because of this, it is surprising to discover that one group of toads, the spadefoot toads, are found in some of the driest desert areas where water is usually scarce. How do these amphibians do it?

AMPHIBIAN: cold-blooded animals that have gills and live in water as young, but breathe air as adults

The tiny spadefoot toad has a small flat spur on each of its rear feet that it can use to dig itself underground and hide from the desert heat. Some toads may burrow 3 feet (1 m) deep. Spadefoot toads, like desert tortoises, can store water inside their body. They can also shed several layers of skin, which then surround them like a waterproof coat so that the moisture in their body doesn't escape into the dry desert soil around them. Buried deep underground, the toads wait, and wait, and wait. They can stay buried for more than a year waiting for the rain to come. The sound of loud summer thunderstorms tells the toads to dig themselves out. When they do, the puddles of water that form after the thunderstorms may last

These spadefoot toads were mating in a temporary puddle. Two weeks later the puddle had dried up.

ECO-Fact

Ten kinds of horned lizards live in the Sonoran Desert. These pretty little lizards rarely bite, and they aren't fast runners so they don't run from their enemies. Instead, they depend on the color of their skin, which matches the ground, to hide. Also, all horned lizards have sharp dagger-like spines on their head, which are meant to discourage snakes and roadrunners from eating them. Some of the lizards use one final trick to save themselves from a hungry predator, such as a kit fox. When the lizard is grabbed it squirts a fine stream of blood out of the corner of its eye. The lizard's blood tastes bad and often causes the predator to drop the lizard, allowing it to escape.

for just a couple of weeks so the toads must hurry. In one night, hundreds of male spadefoot toads pop out of the ground, hop to the puddles, and begin to call loudly. The noise can sometimes be heard a mile (1.6 km) away. Female toads are attracted to the noise and they hop over to find a mate. Within another day or two the toads are finished, the males stop calling, and the puddles are quiet again. It's unclear how long the toads live but likely it is for several years.

The eggs of some spadefoot toads hatch in just 12 hours, which is faster than any other frog or toad, and the tadpoles may grow into tiny pea-size adults in only a week or so. Compare that to the bullfrog, for example, whose tadpole may take two years to grow up and become a frog.

Spadefoot toads need to grow quickly because the desert sun and heat can quickly dry up a puddle and kill the tadpoles before they have time to change into adults. A biologist friend of mine discovered that spadefoot toads raise two kinds of tadpoles that he called "cows" and "wolves." The cows chew on green plants and the wolves chew on each other. The wolf-like tadpoles are larger, have a special mouth for cutting flesh, and they eat dead tadpoles. When the desert puddle in which they live begins to dry up too quickly, the "wolves" may even attack and eat their brothers and sisters. A meat-eating tadpole grows more quickly than a tadpole that eats only green plants. The cannibal toads are nature's way to make sure that at least a few of the tadpoles survive. When the puddle finally dries up, any tiny toads that are still alive dig themselves underground and wait for the next summer rain.

CANNIBAL: an animal that eats its own kind

This is a cluster of spadefoot toad eggs. The growing tadpoles are surrounded by a covering of clear jelly.

PREDATOR
an animal that hunts and kills other animals for food

Worldwide, there are about 5,400 different kinds of mammals. The biggest group of mammals is the rodents, of which there are 2,270 in the world. Most rodents are squirrel-size or smaller, and all of them have large, sharp front teeth. A rodent's front teeth never stop growing throughout its life and it must chew all the time to keep the teeth from growing too large.

Rodents are the most common mammals that live in the desert. As many as nine different kinds may live together in a patch of desert no larger than a football field. The common desert rodents include many species of mice and ground squirrels. There are also kangaroo rats that hop around on their hind feet like the kangaroos in Australia, and tunnel-loving pocket gophers with fur-lined pockets in their cheeks where they carry bits of plants. I think the most comical of the desert rodents is the pack rat, which builds a big pile of dead cactus parts and then lives inside its fortress of spiny plants, protected from its enemies. The funny part about the pack rat is that it likes to collect unusual objects that it finds in the desert, and then store them in its house. Scientists have found such things as keys, watches, coins, aluminum cans, animal bones, dried cow patties, and even a set of false teeth. No one knows why pack rats collect these things.

The kangaroo rat has especially long whiskers.

A female tarantula.

ECO-Fact

Tarantulas (tar-ANN-chew-las) are large, hairy spiders, and some of the ones in the Sonoran Desert are as big as an adult woman's hand. Mostly they hunt at night to avoid the daytime heat of the desert. Because they are large they make an attractive meal for lizards, snakes, elf owls, and screech owls. Tarantulas have an unusual way to protect themselves from an enemy. They flick stinging hairs into its face by rubbing their back legs against their body. The hairs sting the eyes, nose, and mouth of the enemy and give the spider a chance to escape.

All of the desert rodents are small, and the desert is a tough place for a small animal to live. Why? Because small animals have a small body that can overheat very quickly, and a small animal loses water more easily than a large animal does. For these two reasons, most desert rodents hide underground during the day when the temperature is hot. They curl up inside deep burrows, hide under piles of rocks, or escape into the shady cracks in trees and large cactuses. The temperature in a burrow is usually many degrees cooler than outside. Then at night, when the desert air cools, the rodents come outside to move around and search for food.

The antelope ground squirrel commonly eats cactus flowers.

The body of this honey pot ant is swollen with golden nectar.

The antelope ground squirrel looks like a chipmunk because of the white stripe on its side. It is the one desert rodent that is tough enough to come outside in the daytime. I've seen these squirrels feeding on cactus flowers when it was 100°F (38°C) in the shade. They can do this because they are able to let their body temperature rise to a remarkable 110°F (43°C), which would kill most other mammals, including humans. When the small squirrels reach these dangerous body temperatures they run underground into their burrow and spread out on their belly in the cool dirt. This allows the heat to soak into the ground and cools off the squirrel. You might do the same thing on hot summer days when you sit on a cold cement floor to cool yourself off.

ECO·Fact

Ants are easy to watch in the desert because so much of the ground is bare. Ants, like humans, make their living in many different ways. One group is the army ants that attack and kill caterpillars, beetles, termites, and other ants. Another group is the harvester ants that gather seeds. A third group, leaf cutter ants, collect fresh green leaves and use these to grow underground gardens of fungus, which they snip off and eat. My favorite desert ants are the honey pot ants, which gather sweet nectar from flowers. They feed the nectar to other ants in the colony who store the sweet liquid in their stomach, causing it to swell up like a tiny grape. Then when the flowers wilt, the storage ants vomit up the sweet fluid to feed the colony.

CHAPTER FOUR

"Being a nature detective is one of my favorite things to do. It's fun to search the sand for clues to see which animals were moving around during the night. I might discover that a kit fox trotted from one creosote bush to the next, sniffing the holes beneath the bushes for a careless kangaroo rat. In another place I might see where a great horned owl caught a cottontail rabbit just as the rabbit was leaving the safety of its burrow. Or I might find clues that a scorpion caught a spider, or a centipede chased a beetle. Scratches in the sand can tell lots of interesting stories. One of the most exciting mysteries I solved was in the sand dunes of southern California. By reading the tracks in the sand I saw where a sidewinder rattlesnake had buried itself in the sand and waited for a mouse to wander near. When a mouse hopped by, the venomous sidewinder struck and bit it. After striking it, the snake probably waited for a while, then followed the trail of the dying mouse and swallowed the dead animal whole. Afterwards, the sidewinder moved to an animal burrow nearby, where it was sunning itself when I found it. Solving such wildlife mysteries is one of the great rewards of exploring the desert."

SAND DUNE
COUNTRY

WHEN PEOPLE THINK OF DESERTS they often think of sand dunes. Yet, sand dunes cover only a very small part of the Sonoran Desert. In the U.S., the biggest area of dunes is in southern California and is called the Algodones (al-go-DOE-ness, which means "cotton" in Spanish) dunes.

SAND TRAVEL

The sidewinder rattlesnake moves forward by moving sideways. By looping and pulling its body sideways the sidewinder doesn't slip as much in the loose sand and it is able to travel faster than it could if it tried to go straight ahead the way other snakes do. I've run after sidewinders a few times to photograph them in the sand dunes and I can tell you that they move pretty fast. Also, when the snake is sidewinding, only two parts of its body are in contact with the hot sand at any moment so they are less likely to get overheated. Snakes that slither in the usual way have the entire length of their body resting on the sand at all times so they can quickly overheat. This may explain why other snakes that hunt in the dunes hunt only at night when the sand is cooler.

Have you ever tried to walk barefoot in loose sand? First of all, if it's the middle of the day, the sand can be so hot that it burns your feet. Also, if you try to walk quickly you get tired very fast because the loose sand slides beneath your feet, making every step a lot of work. Two animals that live in the sand dunes of the Sonoran Desert solve these problems in an interesting way.

Scientists believe the scaly horns of the sidewinder protect the snake's eyes from injury.

ECO-Fact

Big black beetles, called pinacate (pin-aa-KAH-tay) beetles, are a common sight on the sand dunes. The beetles are often seen in the daytime when few other creatures are moving around. The beetles eat bits of dead plants that get blown onto the dunes. To defend themselves from predators the beetles can't fly away, and they can't sting, scratch, or bite. Instead, they stand on their head with their bottom in the air and squirt out a blob of smelly brown liquid, which most predators dislike.

The fringe-toed lizard is active during the day and eats insects and other small lizards.

The fringe-toed lizard is another sand dune expert. It has long scales on the edge of its rear toes, which work like snowshoes to help the lizard run quickly over soft sand without sinking. The lizard's body has adapted in other ways as well because of the sandy habitat in which it lives. Its head is shaped like a wedge so that it can dive quickly under the sand to escape from enemies, and its body scales are especially smooth so that it can swim easily through the sand as if it was water. The lizard also has earflaps to keep the sand out and a ridge around its eyes to protect them when it is underground. It's a great thrill to watch a fringe-toed lizard race across the sand and then suddenly dive underground and completely disappear.

CREEPY CRAWLIES
OF THE NIGHT

In the daytime, the sand dunes can be a quiet place, but at night, the creepy crawlies come out to search for prey. One of the nighttime creatures is the giant desert centipede that has dozens of legs and can grow up to 8 inches (20 cm) long. Two of the centipede's front feet have venom glands that the fast-moving animal uses to kill beetles, grasshoppers, crickets, spiders, and even rodents, small lizards, and snakes.

The tail of the centipede is shaped and colored like its head. When a centipede is frightened it hides its head under its body and waves its tail around to fool a predator into biting the wrong end. Then if the centipede is grabbed, its head is free to bite back.

The scorpion is another desert critter with a scary reputation. Because of their stinger, many people are frightened of scorpions and so they never get close enough to see how one really looks.

Thus, they think any small creature crawling around the desert sand must be a dangerous scorpion even though it may be completely harmless. One of these harmless animals is the scary-looking wind scorpion, which, despite its name, isn't a true scorpion at all. The wind scorpion is covered with spiky hairs and has four giant fangs at the front of its head. These are common predators in the Sonoran Desert. They chase and kill spiders and insects with great speed, but they couldn't do much harm to us two-legged types.

Another harmless animal with a misleading name is the whipscorpion. It has large claws on its front legs that it uses to crush and tear apart its prey. The whipscorpion gets its name from its long whip-like tail, which scares off its attacker. When a whipscorpion is angry, it can spray a stream of vinegar up to 30 inches (76 cm) away from the tip of its tail. That's why the whipscorpion is sometimes called the vinegarroon (vin-ah-gar-ROON).

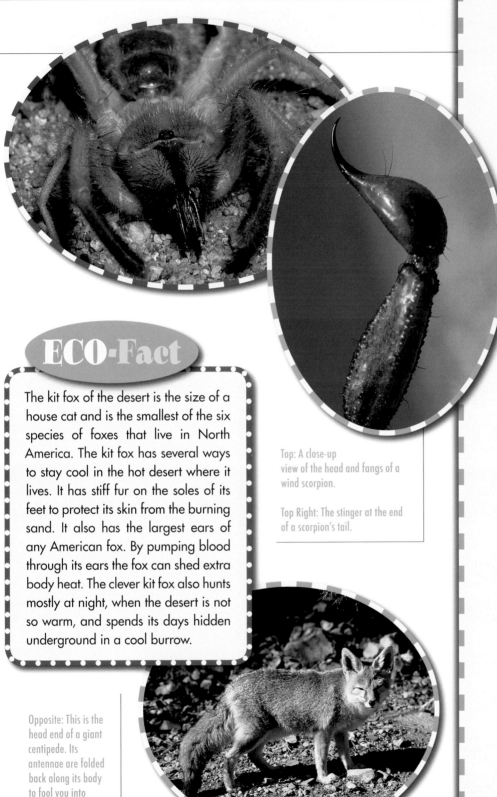

Of course there are real scorpions in the desert, too. In fact, there are about 30 different kinds of scorpions in the Sonoran Desert. All scorpions have a venomous stinger at the tip of their tail, which they use to defend themselves and to kill large prey. But only one, the bark scorpion, is really dangerous to humans. Scorpions do especially well in the dryness of the desert because they can lose almost half the water in their body and still survive. The amazing scorpion can also let its body temperature heat up to 115°F (46°C). Such a high temperature would cook any other desert creature. Scorpions are probably the toughest animal in the desert, which may explain why they've been on earth for more than 400 million years.

ECO-Fact

The kit fox of the desert is the size of a house cat and is the smallest of the six species of foxes that live in North America. The kit fox has several ways to stay cool in the hot desert where it lives. It has stiff fur on the soles of its feet to protect its skin from the burning sand. It also has the largest ears of any American fox. By pumping blood through its ears the fox can shed extra body heat. The clever kit fox also hunts mostly at night, when the desert is not so warm, and spends its days hidden underground in a cool burrow.

Top: A close-up view of the head and fangs of a wind scorpion.

Top Right: The stinger at the end of a scorpion's tail.

Opposite: This is the head end of a giant centipede. Its antennae are folded back along its body to fool you into thinking that you are looking at its tail.

CLOWN OF THE DESERT

In the old West when the stagecoach carried travelers across the desert, the roadrunner would sometimes race beside the horses and outrun them. Anyone who has ever watched a roadrunner sprinting here and there across the desert has to laugh and smile at this feathered clown. Many years ago a famous American scientist and artist, George Miksch Sutton, wrote about his love of the roadrunner. "Watch him race across the sand, full speed, after a lizard. Watch him plunge headfirst

into a clump of cactus, and emerge, whacking his limp victim on the ground. Watch him jerk a slender snake from the grass, fling it into the air, grab it by the head or neck, and gulp it headfirst. Watch him stalk a grasshopper, making a sudden rush with wings and tail fully spread, frightening the doomed insect into flight, then leaping 3 or 4 feet into the air to snatch it in his long bill. Watch the roadrunner for an hour at his daily business of catching food and you will think him the most amazing of all the desert's amazing creatures."

ECO-Alert

In some areas of the desert, motorcycles, dune buggies, and all-terrain vehicles tear up the sand dunes and kill many of the plants that are struggling to grow. The heavy vehicles also collapse animal burrows and crush snakes and lizards hiding under the sand. As well, the noise of these machines often frightens the local birds and animals.

The keen nose of the turkey vulture helps it to find dead animals that were accidentally killed by careless humans.

CHAPTER FIVE

> "I have been interested in owls since I was a boy, and it was the lucky spotting of a rare owl that got me started bird-watching many years ago. One spring I made a special trip to the desert just to search for one kind of owl, the elf owl. The tiny elf owl is no bigger than a sparrow and is the smallest owl in the world. I found a pair nesting inside an old woodpecker hole in a giant saguaro cactus. The female owl was sitting on chicks at the time and her mate was feeding the family crickets, moths, and beetles. As I watched, the male would disappear into the night for 10 to 15 minutes, then fly back to the hole with a meal in his beak and stick his head inside to deliver the treat to his family. One time the male came back with a scorpion that was still wiggling around. Among birds, the tiny elf owl is the greatest scorpion killer of them all. One scientist examined an elf owl that had four scorpions in its stomach, and all of the scorpions had their venomous stingers bitten off. That's one tough bird."

BAJADAS: THE ROCKY SLOPES

BETWEEN THE FLAT ALLUVIAL PLAINS and the foot of the desert mountain chains are rocky gravel slopes, called bajadas. The rocky soil of the bajada is not as fine as it is on the plains so rainwater drains away quickly. The bajada is sometimes called the cactus zone because these spiny plants grow so well here. For me as a photographer, the cactus gardens of the bajadas are the most beautiful face of the Sonoran Desert.

CACTUS CHAMPS

The champions of the cactus gardens are the two giant cactuses, the saguaro and the cardón. The cardón can grow up to 60 feet (18 m) tall and is the largest cactus in the world. This magnificent plant only grows in the Mexican portion of the Sonoran Desert. The tall cactus is a popular place for turkey vultures to perch at sunrise with their wings spread open to soak up the morning heat.

The saguaro and the cardón look very similar. When they are full grown, each has a thick pleated central trunk with six to eight arms branching out from it. The saguaro is shorter than the cardón, but it is still quite tall at 40 to 50 feet (12.2 to 15.3 m). The saguaro is found in Arizona and northern Mexico and is a popular symbol of the Sonoran Desert. There is even a national park named after it, Saguaro National Monument in southeastern Arizona. The saguaro, which has large, pretty white flowers that bloom in May, is the official state flower of Arizona.

On cool nights the body temperature of a turkey vulture drops by several degrees. In the morning the birds use the rays of the sun to warm up again.

The waxy white flowers of the cardón cactus bloom at night to attract bats and night-flying insects, especially moths.

Saguaro cacti of many different ages are growing on this rocky slope.

It's hard to believe that some people get enjoyment by shooting a cactus full of holes with a rifle or handgun. Unfortunately, this happens too often in the desert. The bullet holes don't kill the plant but they allow diseases to get inside the cactus, which may later kill it. This kind of target practice is not only bad for the plant, but can also be dangerous to people. If loosened, the heavy, spine-covered cactus arms could fall and kill a person.

Scientists have studied the saguaro more than any other plant in the Sonoran Desert. What the scientists discovered was that the giant cactus plays a very important role in the life of desert wildlife. Orioles, finches, woodpeckers, doves, and bats feed on the cactus's large white flowers and juicy red fruits. Rodents and rabbits eat saguaro cactuses when they are babies and few tiny saguaros escape the nibbling teeth of these animals.

Even fully-grown saguaros have no way of protecting themselves against the sharp beaks of birds. Luckily, the damage is usually not serious.

Gila woodpeckers and birds called gilded flickers drill nesting holes in the trunks and arms of mature saguaros. The holes don't kill the cactus and a scar forms around the inside of the cavities. The holes provide the woodpeckers with a nesting

ECO-Fact

Seed-eating birds are the most common group of birds living in the desert. This is not surprising when you learn that almost every square foot of desert contains hundreds, and sometimes thousands, of seeds. You can recognize a seed-eating bird from the shape of its beak, which is usually short and stout. The bigger the beak, the larger the seed it can crack. In the desert, the biggest seed-cracking beaks belong to the cardinal and the pyrrhuloxia (pire-ha-LOX-ee-ah).

Both the cardinal above and the pyrrhuloxia on the right are slightly smaller in body size than the backyard robin. Besides eating seeds, both birds eat wild fruits and berries, grasshoppers, beetles, and caterpillars.

OASIS: a rich area in the desert where water is found

place that is safe from most predators, and protects them from the heat and wind outside. The woodpeckers usually drill a new nest hole every year. Old nest holes don't stay empty for long, though. More than 30 different species of desert birds use the abandoned woodpecker nests. They are especially popular with elf owls, kestrels, purple martins, flycatchers, and finches.

Above you can see the four holes woodpeckers have drilled into the trunks of several saguaro cacti. A single trunk may have as many as a dozen holes in it and look like an apartment building for desert birds.

ECO-Fact

When cactuses grow in the open sunshine they can overheat when they are small. This is why many grow in the shade of desert trees and bushes. These are called "nurse trees" because they protect the small cactuses from the sun.

The small banded gecko is active only at night.

When an old saguaro finally dies and falls over it continues to benefit desert animals. This makes it a keystone species for desert wildlife. Many beetles, such as the blue cactus borer, burrow through the dead plant, feeding on its rotting flesh. And other animals, such as lizards called geckos (GEK-coes), snakes, centipedes, and scorpions use the fallen cactus as a perfect desert oasis.

KEYSTONE SPECIES: a plant or animal whose presence benefits many other animals

47

GILA MONSTER

There are more than 60 different kinds of lizards living in the Sonoran Desert. All of them have teeth and feed on other animals, but only one species is venomous—the gila monster. This beautiful pink and black lizard is not a monster at all, just a slow moving desert predator that doesn't want trouble. Even so, it can defend itself forcefully if a person bothers it. Once a gila monster bites, it holds on like a bulldog and chews the venom into the victim. Although its bite is not deadly to humans, the pain and swelling can be severe.

The gila monster, like the desert tortoise, spadefoot toad, and many other desert animals, is typically active for only a very brief time each year. Even though the gila monster is out of winter hibernation from March until November, it may still hide underground in a rocky crevice or inside

a burrow for most of the time throughout the summer. Since a gila monster is not very active, it may eat only a few times each year. Gila monsters prey on rodents, rabbits, ground-nesting birds and their eggs, snakes, lizards, and tortoises. They can eat up to half their body weight in a single meal. So, if a lucky gila monster finds a nest of unlucky newborn cottontail rabbits it may eat the entire litter. Fat is then stored in the lizard's thick tail.

For some people, the handsome gila monster makes an attractive pet. In the past, these lizards were collected so often from the wild that they disappeared from many desert areas. In 1952, the gila monster became the first venomous animal to be legally protected in North America.

THE CACTUS PIG

I don't usually get frightened when I am in the desert alone, but one time when I was walking up a dry wash I got really scared. All of a sudden I heard something crashing through the bushes heading straight toward me. It all happened so fast that I didn't have time to react. Before I knew it three black, pig-like animals came rushing out of the shrubbery. I guess they didn't know I was there because as soon as they saw me they skidded in the dirt, changed course, and raced away grunting.

The animals weren't pigs at all. They were javelinas (have-a-LEEN-ahs), a distant relative of the barnyard pig. It was my first time seeing a javelina in the wild and I remembered reading that they had long, sharp canine teeth that they use to defend themselves when they were cornered or scared. Luckily for me they didn't feel the need to use them.

The javelina is one of the few desert animals that lives in groups. Herds usually contain about a dozen animals and they generally remain within about 15 feet (5 m) of each other. Herd members stay in touch by grunting and sniffing each other.

Javelinas have an area on their back that leaks a musty oil with a strong odor. I could smell it when the three javelinas ran past me in the wash. The animals rub the oil on trees, rocks, and bushes in their home territory to let other javelinas know that this patch of desert belongs to them. Herd members also rub the oil on each other, which is one of their favorite things to do. As a result of all the scent-marking, each herd of javelinas has its own special smell that every member recognizes.

Javelinas have the remarkable ability to eat the spiny pads of prickly pear cactuses, thanks to their unusually tough mouth. In fact, in some desert areas, cactus pads are the only food that javelinas eat and that explains their nickname, cactus pig.

The javelina is about 3 feet (0.9 m) long and stands about 2 feet (0.6 m) tall at its front shoulders. During the cold winter months javelinas are active during the day, but in the heat of summer they rest in the shade in the daytime and feed in the cool of the night.

CHAPTER SIX

"The peregrine falcon is perhaps the fastest bird on wings, reaching speeds over 180 miles per hour (300 kph). This magnificent bird of prey is found all along the desert coastline of Baja, Mexico. One winter day when I hiked into the desert mountains of Baja at sunrise I saw something I never expected to see. A great horned owl was sitting on a rocky ledge eating a peregrine falcon. How had the owl, which is a slowpoke in the air, ever managed to catch the jet-fighter of birds? I'll never know the real answer but I can guess what happened. In the darkness before sunrise the falcon had probably been resting on the cliffs waiting to go hunting for the day. Out of the blackness came the great horned owl, which some people call the night shark, and with its deadly talons it likely grabbed the falcon before it had a chance to react. Even the mightiest of hunters can end up as breakfast."

DESERT MOUNTAINS

IMAGINE THAT YOU ARE AN astronaut drifting high above the earth inside the space shuttle. As the shuttle flies over the Sonoran Desert you look out the window and see the many small mountain chains scattered throughout the desert. Some of the mountain chains are short and others are long, but they all run in same direction, pointing toward Canada. It's been said the mountain chains look like an army of caterpillars marching north.

No matter where you stand in the Sonoran Desert, mountains are visible in the distance. Most of the mountains are less than 5,000 feet (1,524 m) high, and desert plants grow right up to the top of them. A few of the mountains rise above 8,000 feet (2,438 m), such as Mount Lemmon in the Santa Catalina Mountains north of Tucson, Arizona, which rises to 9,157 feet (2,791 m). At the top of the tallest mountains there are forests of evergreen trees that look more like northern Canada than the Sonoran Desert. However, the smaller mountains are covered with desert plants, and there are many fascinating animals that make their home in this rocky terrain.

The desert mountains are a difficult habitat for wildlife to live in. Water in these mountains is even scarcer than in the bajadas and alluvial plains below. Also, the winds can be strong, which dries out the land even more and the creatures that live there can get really thirsty. One advantage that the mountains offer is safety from predators. High cliffs are a good nesting place for eagles, hawks, vultures, and ravens, as well as many smaller birds, including swallows and swifts. Also, many desert mountains are covered with caves where bobcats, mountain lions, ringtails, foxes, skunks, and many other animals can hide from the heat and sun of the desert below. Hike up any desert mountain and you will probably make some exciting wildlife discoveries.

The large powerful mountain lion above specializes in hunting deer, bighorn sheep, and javelinas. The smaller bobcat hunts desert cottontails, jack rabbits, rodents, snakes, and birds.

Ravens sometimes use the strong winds in desert mountains to play and chase each other, as these birds were doing.

RINGTAILS
AND COATIS

Everyone knows the raccoon. But did you know that two of the raccoon's closest relatives live in the Sonoran Desert? Few people know about them because they are rarely seen. These overlooked desert relatives are the ringtail and the coati (ko-AH-tee) and they live in the mountains of the desert.

The ringtail can rotate its hind feet so they face backward. This lets a ringtail climb down cliffs and trees head first. Male and female ringtails live alone for much of the year and only come together for a few days in late spring when they mate. Mothers raise their 2 to 4 young by themselves.

The ringtail was chosen by school children to be the official state mammal of Arizona. It may seem like a funny choice since the ringtail is a shy animal that only comes out at night. But look at a photograph of a ringtail and you'll immediately know why the children chose it. The ringtail has a long black-and-white tail, large black eyes, big round ears, and a little white face that looks like a fox. In short, the ringtail looks cute and cuddly. The ringtail, however, is a predator. It eats birds and their eggs, pack rats and mice, lizards and snakes.

The coati is larger than the ringtail and is a recent immigrant to the deserts of the United States. It wandered across the Mexican border into the U.S. less than a hundred years ago. The coati looks as if it were made from the parts of other animals. It has the nose of a javelina, the face of a badger, and the tail of a raccoon.

The coati, like the javelina, travels in groups. As many as 30 of them may wander together through the canyons in the mountains. They dig in the dirt and leaves with their nose to search for roots, beetles, and crickets. They also eat cactus fruit, lizards, snakes, and rodents. Coatis are scavengers, too, and will eat any dead animal they happen to find. In the desert where food can be scarce, it doesn't pay to be a fussy eater.

Coatis are active during the day and spend the night in caves and trees.

CLIFF DWELLERS

Drawings of the bighorn sheep were often painted and scratched into the rocks of the mountains by the early Indians who lived in the desert. For them, the sheep was an animal to admire and an important animal to hunt. There are many reasons to admire the desert bighorn. It can go for weeks without drinking, and it can survive on the water it gets from the dried grasses and plants it eats. Then, when it finds a water hole, it can drink up to 4 gallons (15 l) of water at one time. That's like drinking 16 quarts (15 l) of milk without stopping. The bighorn can also let its body heat up to 107°F (42°C) in the daytime, then at night release the heat to the cool desert air. A human would die at such a high body temperature. The sheep can also lose three times as much body water as a human can and still survive.

ECO-Fact

The cliff swallow builds a round nest of mud attached to the face of a cliff. The average nest takes about a week or two to build and consists of about 1,000 mouthfuls of mud. Several thousand pairs of swallows may nest together in a single large colony.

On my last trip to the Sonoran Desert I spotted a band of bighorns resting on some steep mountain cliffs. I decided to climb up to them for a closer look. I'm sure the sheep saw me coming from far away but they stayed calm and didn't run. They probably felt safe on their high rocky ledges. After 30 minutes of climbing I was getting pretty close. The female leader of the band suddenly decided I had gotten close enough. Like Spiderman she leaped from one narrow rock ledge to another with the others following closely behind her. The speed and ease with which she ran across the face of the cliff was truly amazing. I could see then why the early desert Indians admired these animals so much.

The bighorn sheep and other desert wildlife live in a different world than we do. It is a world we are only beginning to understand. I feel very lucky to have visited the Sonoran Desert many times to watch the wildlife that lives there. I remember laughing as a swarm of ants struggled to squeeze a large red flower through the tiny entrance to their colony. Another time I watched three young ground squirrels chase each other in a continuous game of tag. Then there was the brave cactus wren that I saw building a nest of sticks in a prickly cholla cactus and wondered how it kept from getting stabbed. Most of all I will never forget the many times I walked in the desert in the last hours of daylight and listened to the soft calling of the doves and quail. I hope some day you also have a chance to wander in the Sonoran Desert and listen to the peaceful voice of nature.

If you want to learn more about the Sonoran Desert and the wildlife that lives there you can search the Internet for the web sites I have listed below. This is where you can learn about the problems facing the desert, what people are doing to save it, and how you can help.

Algodones Dunes, California
http://www.americansouthwest.net/california/algodones_dunes/

Anza Borrego State Park, California
http://www.parks.ca.gov/default.asp?page_id=638

Cabeza Prieta National Wildlife Refuge, Arizona
http://www.fws.gov/southwest/refuges/Arizona/cabeza.html

Catalina State Park, Arizona
http://www.azstateparks.com/Parks/CATA/index.html

Coalition for Sonoran Desert Protection, Arizona
http://www.sonorandesert.org/

Desert Tortoise Natural Area, California
http://www.blm.gov/ca/st/en/prog/wildlife/watchable/wf_lister/desert_tortoise.html

Kofa National Wildlife Refuge, Arizona
http://www.fws.gov/Refuges/profiles/index.cfm?id=22570

Organ Pipe Cactus National Monument, Arizona
http://www.nps.gov/orpi/

Pinacate National Park, Mexico
http://www.parksinperil.org/wherewework/mexico/protectedarea/elpinacate.html

Saguaro National Monument, Arizona
http://www.nps.gov/sagu/

When DR. WAYNE LYNCH met AUBREY LANG, he was an emergency doctor and she was a pediatric nurse. Within 5 years they were married and had left their jobs in medicine to work together as writers and wildlife photographers. For more than 30 years they have explored the great wilderness areas of the world.

Dr. Lynch is a popular guest lecturer and an award-winning science writer. His books cover a wide range of subjects, including the biology and behavior of owls, penguins, and northern bears; arctic, boreal, and grassland ecology; and the lives of prairie birds and mountain wildlife. He is a Fellow of the internationally recognized Explorers Club, and an elected Fellow of the prestigious Arctic Institute of North America.

Dr. Lynch has written the texts and taken the photographs for five titles in NorthWord's Our Wild World animal series: *Seals, Hawks, Owls, Vultures,* and *Falcons.* He is also the author and photographer of *The Arctic, The Everglades, Prairie Grasslands,* and *Rocky Mountains* from the Our Wild World Ecosystems series.